MY AMERICAN PARTNER

HOW TO OBTAIN AND KEEP AMERICAN DECISION MAKERS

Other Works by the Author

1. East Over West
    A unique work which unveiled the mutual influence of the
    far eastern art over the western world of art and vice versa.

2. The Pantheon of the Greek and Roman Gods
    A fascinating spectrum of gods and beliefs during the
    period of the two ancient empires.

MY AMERICAN PARTNER

HOW TO OBTAIN AND KEEP AMERICAN DECISION
MAKERS

JACOB EYAL Ph.d.

authorHOUSE®

AuthorHouse™ LLC
1663 Liberty Drive
Bloomington, IN 47403
www.authorhouse.com
Phone: 1-800-839-8640

Published by AuthorHouse 05/13/2014

ISBN: 978-1-4918-7393-9 (sc)
ISBN: 978-1-4918-7392-2 (e)

Library of Congress Control Number: 2014905077

"Mr. Jack how can I start business with an American importer . . . I have a great idea about my product, can you tell me how to find a buyer."

All you need is a trustful counter-partner.

CONTENTS

ABOUT THE BOOK

This book was written to provide you, the new entrepreneur, with the tools and skills to reach the American Market and to gain a business partner (buyer). Now-a-days, as we all are aware of, China has become the manufacturer powerhouse of the globe, while the United States maintains—by the virtue of its richness, the ultimate most powerful product consuming market.

Naturally, to conduct successful business between these two giants (Trade Avenue) is the highest desire sought after by all trade businessmen.

Through 25 years of trade negotiation with the Chinese manufacturers and the US buyers, I have been often approached by young Chinese people who are eager to seize opportunity to open a trade channel with an American counter-part.

If you have the entrepreneurial bent and the integrity it requires—this book will provide you with indispensable ideas and will lead you step by step to your desire goal.

The Chinese are notorious of being suspicious about foreigners who have been called "people from over the mountain." Let me inform you that your American counter-part is just as insecure and hesitant when he is approached by a business man from China. The suspicion derives from the lack of knowledge about the Orient and its People. It is up to you to implement tactics that eliminate those obscure feelings.

Any product can be sold to the American Market, yet the more promising result will be at the hands of those who find a niche in any given industry. Absolutely, it is a challenging mission and a well rewarding one. Having said that, bear in mind, that the low end products now-a-days will be a dead end avenue for any new comer, since the huge American corporations like office depot, home depot, and particularly Wal-Mart are dominating the low end market and it is almost impossible to compete with them, neither can you join them providing you financial and operation structure are too limited. Therefore the better policy for you to take is shooting towards products which sell in the mid-range products that cover a wide spectrum of the prospective buyers; or higher end products targeting a smaller market share with higher profit expectation.

"A bird does not sing because it has an answer, it sings because it has a song."

Chinese Proverb

Chapter 1

Initial Preparations

"He who is best prepared can best serve his moment of inspiration."

Samuel Taylor Coleridge

Finding the Right Product

Any product can be sold to the American Market, yet the more promising result will be in the hands of those who find a niche in any given industry. It is absolutely a challenging mission and a well rewarding one.

- ☐ Stay away from low end products. It is dead end avenue. The huge American corporate such as Office Depot, Home Depot, and particularly Wal-Mart already dominate the market. Low end products dictate a thin profit.

- ☐ Avoid those products which demand a find touch and high quality. Providing you have no experience and high end products usually being support by a brand-name which you cannot provide, not yet.

- ☐ Target your products to the middle class American market. This wide range consuming arena embraces any size of operation. Any kinf of product, at any part od the U.S. market and by the end of the day it promises substantial level of profit.

"If you do not climb the mountain, you will not see the plain."

Chinese Proverb

Know Your Competitors

Although your product may have a clean advantage on the current product in the hands of your competitors; remember, the dynamic of the trade is inventing itself constantly.

- ☐ Investigate among your colleagues, friends, and family members about those companies who import same or similar products. Inquire about their headquarters in the U.S.

- ☐ Find out the way your competitors pack and ship the goods. Unveil the final destination point. This inside information will supply you with indispensable clues in your way to determine what part of the market to address territorial wise.

- ☐ Collect information per the price they pay through individual who works in that manufacture plain. Learn about the quality they ship the goods per week on month and discover the diversity of their styles.

"Confidence is that feeling by which the mind embraces on great and honorable courses with a sure hope and trust in itself."

Cicero

Be Mentally Prepared

On your way to open the window of opportunity there are two core aspects you must maintain at its highest level:
-   High Self Esteem.
-   The spirit of the entrepreneur.

Develop the inner power to tell yourself that you can di it!

☐   The ultimate source for high self-esteem is your knowledge. Knowledge about your products, the competitor's product, the counterpart and the market behavior.

☐   The spirit of the entrepreneur means to maintain the power to take risks. Gearing toward a great achievement may end up in a hard failure, however this possibility should not hold you from target yourself to the highest goal.

☐   Dare to challenge your life while overcoming the fear of lose. For stagnating in a familiar alley lacking the entrepreneur vision, while changing the course elevating the spirit.

☐   Keep a distance from the mediocre who lacks the courage or the spirit to walk through unfamiliar territory.

"When you drink water, remember the source."

Chinese Proverb

Read About the U.S.

Knowing about America will give you great deal of advantage and strength on your way to the partnership journey. On the other hand, being ignorant about the basic facts which drive the American society, its history, geography, and the essence of its culture will put you under a negative light.

☐ Come to know with the American geography and demography—in particular with the area (the city, the region, etc.) where you are about to conduct your business venture.

☐ Knowing its size will influence the logistic of the goods shipment and will teach about the purchasing power of its population and the type of products which appeal there.

☐ Learn about the American holidays and national days so your calling will not be answered by stubborn answering machines, let alone arriving when everywhere is closed.

☐ Earn the respect of your partners by being acquainted with the American value: its democracy, culture, religions, politics, etc. Remember, a short way to build the essential rapport is by sharing what is important for the other side.

"A book holds a house of gold.

Chinese Proverb

Learn About the Local

Being a vast nation, each of its fifty states maintains its own unique identity. You will find this more so in the large states, like California, New York, Texas, which have distinct differences state to state and city to city.

☐ Knowing the city/town population and pace of life will channel your business expectations to a more realistic one.

☐ On your way to conduct business in a certain city you will gain a great advantage by discovering its major wholesale and retails contents—in particular those centers which specialize in trading with the product you are interested in developing.

Chapter 2

Target the Market

"Define your business goals clearly so that others can see them as you do."

George F. Burns

The U.S. Market Infrastructure

The American market is fast and diversified. However the infrastructure can be characterized divided in 4 major identities:

The Manufacture

☐ The Manufacture produces the goods whether within the country or overseas (or both).

☐ The manufacture offers the produced goods to the market usually thru the distributors or the numbers of distributors.

☐ In essence any manufacture who produces similar products to yours—maintain a direct competition and challenge your existence.

☐ Being sizable operation the manufacture lacks the flexibility you have.

☐ The manufacture often offers credit line to its clients.

"There is less to fear from outside competition than from inside inefficiency, discourtesy, and bad service."

Anonymous

The Distributor

This separation is rooted—in most cases—into three generations back at the time when American manufactures set their marketing infrastructure solely on distributing channels.

☐ The distributors ownership maintained in the hand of inheritors who together with an investing institute succeeded in gaining the trust and the confidence of the supplier/manufactures and strengthen its grip at the given distribution territory and beyond.

☐ This noticeable size of operation is the main player for your specific industry in a given territory—one or multiple states. His obligation history to the local manufacture will leave you with a very slim chance to perform as a new vendor for his operation.

☐ The distributor is the spoil child of the business. He gets the newest products and distributes it among wholesalers and dealers while maintaining a profit of 30-40 percent above the purchasing price. In addition, he grants preferable terms of payment.

"In the end all business operations can be reduced to three words: people, product, and profits."

Lee Iaccoca

The Wholesaler

Through my extensive years of experience with the American market—the whole link in the chain of the trade is most suitable for the new comer in any given industry.

- [ ] This is considered rather a small business operation manager and controlled by a small group of professional individuals. Usually they are hand people highly motivated rich in experience and are open to new ventures—whether it be a new vender or a new product.

- [ ] The wholesaler is the body who covers a relatively small territory and can receive goods from the manufacture and the distributors.

- [ ] In many cases it is an operation which is conducted by family members who continue what has been founded on a previous generation. The key person for you the new vendor is the inheritor who is relatively young and lack of experience. Often he is willing to hear about new products, technology, or partnership.

- [ ] The wholesaler prime clients are the dealers which are operating in a relatively small geographic area, most command in a preset radius of about 100 or so miles within one state.

"Arriving at one goal is the starting point of another."

John Dewey

The Dealer

A small size business operated by a middle class American. An individual who insist to be self-employed and the one who looked for a niche in certain shopping mall, put together a moderate investment and hired 3 to 5 mediocre to assist him-her.

☐ The dealer is actually the owner of the store or couple of them in the vicinity of a certain metropolis.

☐ The dealer is approached by one or several state or the regions distributors as well as the wholesalers operations. He is choosy and rarely loyal to any supplier. In most cases he dictates the terms of payment and keeps the right to return the goods in a very capricious manner.

☐ He receives wide spectrum of products plus display accessories. He reaps the lion share in the market to offer the goods to the end users in a substantial profit margin of 100 percent and more.

Chapter 3

How to Find
Prospective Buyers

Nothing is gut without.”

Psalm

Reach For Formal Information

As stated before, you can sell *any* product in the U.S. but you cannot sell it to *everyone*. To find a prospective buyer who will respond to your business partnership offer—the one who will appreciate your product and personality—is on of the hardest missions.

☐ Conduct research information relating to the industry which withholds the product you ask to trade with in the U.S market. Be very specific. Try to define the exact category in the industry you have decided to work with. Any deviation to discover greater part of that industry will get you out of focus and will end up in weakening your move.

☐ Look for objective yet professional publication which circulate through American Chamber of Commerce located in any major city. These publications whether they are special magazines, survey reports or news circulating revealing new products, new sources, etc.

☐ Collect information which revels the essential details per the companies who conduct business with similar products to the one you are about to launch. Be through in learning the major players in the industry our about to join—in both sides of the trade—the manufactures as well as the importers.

☐ Browse through the trade magazines which relate to the objective industry. Pick up the major names and their headquarters location in the U.S, This information will build your geographic orientation and target your inquiry toward the most potential area for your product to be accepted,

"He who would learn to fly one day must first learn to stand and walk and run and climb and dance: one can't fly into flying."

Friedrich Nietzche

Direct Information

In our era of electronic communication, the internet provides the ultimate source to go by. Browsing thru the unlimited pages of information will lead you to overcome the geographical barrier and enable you to draw very specific information about any industry at any city and town of the U.S.

☐ Remember: obtaining common information about companies in the states and its official buyers names is a legal act. Furthermore, inquiring about the decision maker, his office time, his phone number, fax number, and email address is perfectly fine.

☐ Use the internet to the best it offers. Getting into Google or Yahoo search engines and browsing through enormous number of companies in any given industry the prospective wholesalers will pop out at your screen will all the relevant information.

☐ Search thoroughly until you find ultimate objective: the decision maker in any company (providing it's a wholesaler) in addition to its location, size of the operation, and the variety of products it sells.

☐ Go beyond the immediate details of that company and discover that company and discover further details such as vendors it buys from, the customers they serve and the territory its operation covers. This vital information will give you an immense competitive advantage.

"I know the price of success: Dedication, hard work, and an unremitting devotion to the things you want to see happen."

Frank Lloyd Wright

Benchmarks for a Meeting
(How to Secure an Appointment)

Providing you have managed to find the prospective buyer which may fit your entry to the import / export trade in the U.S. market—the next vital and critical step is to contact him and get this interest to meet with you.

□ Make sure to meet with the person who has the authority to say yes or no. Having a meeting==gin with anyone else besides the person with the decision power will end the meeting with fruitless results.

□ The more decision makers you meet the true counterpart you gain which lead eventually to more business transactions.

□ Insist on getting a persona land official meeting. Any substitute for face to face meeting—in most cases is a recipe for failure. For when you meet someone face to face you can hear him and see him at the same time and the result is by far more promising and more productive.

□ Prepare to stand tall in front of any person who may greet you in his office hence there is no individual American more powerful than your sincere and firm will.

□ Reject and suggestion by the prospective buyer to send his samples of your product before a personal meeting. Countless product samples have been sent by me at early stages of my business journey in almost all cases; the buyer ignored the package or just did not find the time to examine what had been sent. There is a greater likelihood that even if he does find time to look at the product, a lot of information had been left untold and the samples will be disregarded.

"Be not afraid of growing slowly; be afraid only if standing still."

Confucius

How to Approach

Prior to the actual cold-call to the prospective counterpart you need to prepare. First designate 2 hours without any distractions from any outside surroundings. Prearrange to ignore incoming calls, eating, drinking, or conversations with other people. Concentrate on the words you are going to use as an introduction. Be ready to answer any question with the appropriate answer and have the conclusion sentence in front of you.

- ☐ A sincere approach is recommended in an contact. Bring your message straight forward.

- ☐ Call the prospective buyer by his first name (it is common U.S. business relations to be informal and also by calling him by his first name, you do not put yourself in a subservient position).

- ☐ Introduce yourself the right way by giving your first name and surname, your company's name as possible. Keep in mind that any foreign language to the American ears is hard to digest, let alone the Chinese name with a Chinese accent.

- ☐ In calling on the decision maker you actually step into the first part of your meeting. Even though it is verbal contact you actually maintain a handshake with your future partner. Your initial call carries the potential to open the door or have it shut for good.

- ☐ Bear in mind that behind an company—being as huge as it is— there is an ordinary person who needs the vendors help in order to fulfill his objective. Therefore, relate to him as an equal partner. Ask as far as you expect to give.

- ☐ A counterpart who wants your product is more product educated customer and will be a better counterpart for the long run.

"River and mountains are more easily changed than man's nature."

Chinese Proverbs (35)

Knowing Your Typical American Buyer

As in most cases the buyer or the purchasing officer in a midsize American company, he is a typical middle class American in his late 40's and an experienced individual, a veteran of a few companies.

- ☐ He is a friendly person yet suspicious and cynical.

- ☐ Although lacking a formal education, he maintains a basic understanding in merchandise cost evaluation.

- ☐ The buyer is an overweight family oriented man who lives in the suburbs of a big city and a baseball fan.

- ☐ He controls the companies buying inventory and that means a huge monetary sum passes through his desk without much left for him besides the power—the power to choose and compose the purchase list. The authority that was put in his hand is actually the substitute for his moderate compensation.

- ☐ That person, except for participating in national trade shows he hardly travels outside his immediate territory. Let alone discovering other countries.

- ☐ He is a typical middle class American, yet innocent of any pretentiousness, guiltless of ambition and a risk-free employee, unsophisticated and ina way naïve to a great extent.

- ☐ He is poorly dressed and he is one who cannot be blamed for a good taste.

- ☐ When the time is right, meaning when you have developed a friendly relationship, this typical buyer would love to be treated to a free lunch (don't dare go beyond that).

"He who every morning plans the transaction of the day
follows that pan carries thread that will guide him through the
labyrinth of the most busy life."

Victor Hugo

The Element of Timing

Calling on your prospective counterpart at the appropriate timing can be a crucial move. Hence the buyer is not waiting for your call which interrupting his current work—consider the middle of the week and middle of the morning as the most relevant timing.

☐ Avoid calling at the early hours of Mondays, the counterpart will be least receptive.

☐ By the same token, do not call on the prospective counterpart 2 minutes before the weekend starts since people are already tuned into the nearest bar for a drink (beer or two to mark the end of a hard working week).

☐ Providing you have searched for the national trade shows calendar in the given industry, avoid calling close to the event since the buyer will not make a move to purchase new products before checking what the trade fair has to offer.

☐ Call the prospective counterpart when you are at your highest level of energy hence calling with a tired voice will not reveal the message you aimed to and the buyer will lose interest rather fast.

☐ Focus on whatever you are about to reveal in your message and refrain from doing anything which may avery your concentration.

"You can surmount the obstacles in your path if you are determined, courageous and hard-working, never be fainthearted. Be resolute but never bitter . . . Permit no one to dissuade you from pursuing the goals you set for yourselves."

Ralph J. Bunche

The Gate Keeper

Before reaching to the extension of the prospective counterpart you will have to pass through the gate keeper: the receptionist or the secretary, or both. This person is rarely open or chatty. In most cases she has developed a cold and even nasty attitude which she cannot be blamed for. Dealing with hundreds of calls per day becomes annoying to deal with.

☐ Do not hate her—you need her, or restrict her courteously just out smart her with a simple yet polite approach. Develop a polite tactic by which to circumvent her and to accomplish your objective.

☐ In those cases where you do not know the name of the buyer or the decision maker, just ask the gate keeper the name of that person, pretending you have to forward him some literature, documents, samples, etc. A far better chance the gate keeper will provide you with his name.

☐ Once you have determined his name, just ask to speak to him—without asking for any favor and without any apologetic vocabulary. Remember the prospective counterpart needs you as much as you need him.

☐ In those events where you know the name of the prospective counterpart who is the decision maker of the company, just ask for him or his extension.

☐ Don't ever accept the suggestion to leave a voicemail. The prospective buyer does not know you from Adam.

"He who is outside the door has already a good part of his journey behind him."

Dutch Proverbs

Chapter 4

Trip Preparation

"Luck favors the mind that is prepared."

Louis Pasteur

Trip Preparation

Once an official business meeting has been obtained with the officer with authority, two issues should immediately be address: the itinerary and the hotel reservation. Although traveling to the U.S. on a business trip which includes air ticket, a good hotel, meals, and ground transportation can be very expensive, maintaining the meeting face to face with the prospective counterpart is essential to development of your business.

☐ Select a reliable airline who maintain routinely air-trip to the U.S. (Air China, Korean Air, China Airlines, Japan Air, Cathey Airlines). Choosing a reliable airline will minimize the surprise of cancellations or delays.

☐ It is imperative to purchase a business class ticket, although the ticket price if far more expensive, you can consider the extra payment as part of your investment.

☐ Make sure you rest during the flight even for a few hours. No matter what you will end up in jet lag. The more you sleep and rest during you hours daytime the more you will be prepared for the time changes.

☐ Bear in mind that you need to be in the prospective counterparts meeting place at least 24 hours prior to the D-date. Getting ready for the current weather and reasonably adjusted to the local timing is necessary to the clear set of mind you need during the meeting.

"The wisdom of life consists in the elimination of nonessentials."

Lin Yutang

What To Take With You

The most important item to take with you on a business trip are samples of your product or service literature. More so, these samples should be in outstanding condition since they are the ones which convince your prospective contra part.

☐ Take your product or services literature in a small quantity/ size and in perfect presentation condition. Each item should be packed individually and in its original box, carton, etc.

☐ Make sure those samples are reflecting the actual product once it leaves the manufacture.

☐ Label each item clearly and itemize with accurateness to the relevant literature. Enclose the specification information: sizes, weights, packing measurements, etc. The more details you supply, the more professional you look.

☐ If the product cannot be presented but thru literature, get a new clean binder while the literature material setting in order inside a company as much information as needed in order to present all that is needed to show your product or service.

☐ Make sure you equip yourself with very good written material, and a fine pen. Having a writing instrument that looks poor creates an embarrassing moment.

☐ The binder and the rest of the written paper plus your valuable items should be contained into a distinguished, fashionable, leather handbag.

"A man is judged by his clothes, a horse by its saddle."

Chinese Proverbs (64)

Clothing

Besides the importance of the appropriate clothing which dictates and adjusts by the weather you are about to confront with, the right attire plays a significant part of the business meeting. By dressing respectively you are signaling to your counterpart that he or she is important to you.

☐ Dress in the code that dictates the American business world. Black and Navy dominate the clothes color. Hence they are considered power colors that build credibility.

☐ Avoid dressing overwhelmingly as a flamboyant so your spear the immediate resentment.

☐ Subdue any invention to appear in shabby clothes which most likely draw a bad impression and in some instances will categorize you as a unorganized person.

☐ Adjust your level of quality in your clothes a bit more than the fashion your counterpart feels comfortable in. Maintaining this approach will signal to the counterpart that you are one of "the team".

☐ Invest into a new suite where your image is built upon.

☐ Overcome the common phenomenon to see Chinese business man dressed up while wearing scruffy shoes. Your shoes are part of your attire—invest in a fashion and quality pair. Walk tall.

☐ One can catch a raining day at any given time in the U.S. Prepare a reliable umbrella and a light rain coat in your immediate arm reach.

"Traveling is a brutality, it forces you to trust strangers and to lose sight of all that familiar comfort of home and friends, you are constantly off balance."

Cesare Pavese

Arriving A Day In Advance

Providing that your meeting destination is in the middle of the states—there is most likely a couple of stops, which compromise a full journey of 30 hours or above from your house to the hotel. By that time you are completely washed out. No matter how many hours you have slept on the place—your body is exhausted, your eyes are red, your mind is out of focus—and the jet lag is taking a toll.

☐ Avoid at any expense to make your way from the airport to the meeting for it is a recipe to sabotage your entire trip's objective. Give yourself some time to recuperate and get oriented.

☐ Designate a full day at the meeting location prior to the actual meeting to provide you enough time to find your way in the new world. The weather, the people.

☐ Rest in your hotel for a couple of hours while checking on the local to three stores (through the yellow pages) which offer similar products you are dealing with.

☐ Take a taxi (avoid public transportation) to these stores and check the competitors' products per their quality. Examine prices, their vendors and learn about the level of satisfaction per their service. Gather as much information as possible—it will teach you about the competition you are facing and how to elevate your advantage.

☐ Purchase a local newspaper and learn about the main sport events in town, You cannot imagine how warmly you will be received when you throw at the beginning of the meeting something like "so the red sox did it again?".

"The real difference between men is energy."

Thomas Fuller

To The Meeting

Groom yourself in the morning and get yourself excited. Assuming you have checked the night before find out the reliable estimation about how long it will take you to drive to your meeting.

- ☐ Refrain from smoking the morning of the meeting and if possible during your entire trip to the U.S. Plan to take a taxi to your partners office. Even though it is considered expensive just add it onto your ticket price.

- ☐ Do not take public transportation—you might end up missing the exact address, arrive late on top of sweating with dress in such disarray as if they have been involved in a fist fight.

- ☐ Make sure to arrive on time from the counterparts stand point it's sacred value. Remember, you will never get a second chance to correct the first impression.

- ☐ Greet the person at the front desk with a smile hand over your business card while providing your name as clearly as possible and the name of the person you are about to meet.

- ☐ Accept any response from the front desk person with patience and gratitude.

- ☐ Prepare to wait longer than expected. Be patient he knows you are there waiting. The longer you wait the better listening he would pay to your presentation.

- ☐ Wait while reading the companies literature; it will help you access its size, policy, economical strengths, etc.

"If you have the will to win, you have achieved half your success; if you don't you have achieved half your failure."

David V.A Ambrose

Chapter 5

At The Meeting

At The Meeting

The next thirty to sixty minutes will determine your success
or failure to find an established business partner. Relate to the
upcoming encounter with the companies buyer as the one and only
opportunity to sell your product. After all the preparations that
have been done, you are on the stage to give the very best show.

☐ Greet your counterpart with a smile, shake hands properly and
coordinate it with words of greeting like "Hi, James Chung,
nice to meet you". This will radiate your friendship and your
warm personality.

☐ Be aware that the oriental business peoples hard of handle
attitude having tendency to shake in a noodle soft manner,
forget this habit, just give a firm handshake and look straight
into his eyes.

☐ Pronounce your first and last name as clearly as possible,
there is no room for bowing as some oriental sales persons are
accustomed too.

☐ Understand the act: the counterpart leads you next to his leaded
desk, he signals no need for product samples to be presented.
He is short and direct. Instead concentrate on asking the
appropriate questions about his company and its current needs
for a product similar to yours.

☐ Explain in detail what is the advantage your product maintains
and the benefit to the counterpart once he purchases it.

"I know that things are goods: friendship and work and conversation."

Rupert Brook

Friendly Buyer

When you are greeted with a sincere smile and a firm hand shake and have been offered to a designated area a large space in which to present your product—you are facing a relationship oriented person who respects the effort for facing that trip.

☐ Take your time. Build a friendly atmosphere, thank him for receiving you and start with a positive comment per his company's location, his office and its size, etc.

☐ Relate to your natives region in case it's been asked in a vague geographical description. (The American counterpart hardly knows over two cities in China).

☐ Be observant—through the picture of his family on the back of his desk or photo from a local sport event will reveal his mentality.

☐ Act with tact—do not comment on the counterparts family reflected from the picture. The American keep their family as an exterritorial identity.

☐ Exchange business cards. Read thoroughly into it and only then put it in your notebook.

☐ Practice the following success proven practice: Encourage the counterpart to talk about his company—ask probing questions (those questions should be written in your notebook, look ahead) and only after collecting desirable information start to describe your product and its advantages.

☐ Listen explicitly without interrupting. For interrupting your counterpart is rude and may prevent him from revealing further valuable and essential information.

"Nothing is so contagious as enthusiasm; it moves stones, it charms brutes. Enthusiasm is the genius of sincerity and truth accomplishes no victories without it."

Edward Bulwen Lytton

Praise Your Product / Service

Providing you have put in order all the benchmarks to support the advantages of tour product/service:

- [ ] Start your presentation with enthusiastic voice, capture your counterpart's attention. Looking at him in the eyes to inspire.

- [ ] Demonstrate the superior profitability your counterpart will gain in comparison to the competition after all—the profit margin plays the bigger role in front of the decision maker.

- [ ] Remembers: Comparison can exist only if you put "apple to apple", material to material and size to size. If only one ingredient is missing, the entire comparison becomes invalid.

- [ ] Advocate your product and its value only after you make sure that these values are relevant in your counterparts operation and never add negative words about the counterparts previous choice he made.

- [ ] Share commensurate information with your counterpart by doing that you enhance your credibility and for a channel to develop a sense of your being an important source for his as well as a sincere one.

- [ ] Bring up a few of your best products and praise its favorable prices, quality, design, and emphasize the uncompromised service it provides with. Read quotation, spec, lead time, and alike from a well prepared notebook.

"Let us go singing as far as we go, the road will be less tedious."

Virgil

Release Relevant Information

The essential points about your company: its location, nature of business (exports to what countries), your number of years in the business, the production capacity, the quality orientation, and the price structure.

☐ The location: Give a brief description about where the manufacture is located. "20 miles north of Shanghai" will be more than enough. Do not bother to disclose the exact location of the small town.

☐ Duration of business: Indicate the number of years you or the factory you are representing have engaged in business. If the number of years is impressive (5-15 years) emphasize it with proud voice. Obviously the longer you conduct business the more serious partners would be considered. IN case the operation is in act only a few years or even months, you would rather avoid mentioning it.

☐ Production capacity: Bring up relevant number as per how units, square foot container the factory produced at the early stage compared to the current capacity. Providing the numbers show a significant increase. And finally present the projection of growth for the next year.

☐ Be realistic with the numbers and accurate details which should be related to your estimation based on the market strength and of course your success level of your company would bring along new customers of his caliber.

"It is by losing himself in the objective, inquiry, creation, and craft, that a man becomes something."

Paul Goodman

The Quality Topic

You will be surprised to discover that the most important issue is not the price of your product but the quality and the ability to sustain that level - in order words, to maintain consistency. More so, many time a low price or suspicion of being an inferior product.

- [ ] Elaborate in details about your quality control method and expressing the obligation to high quality products. You can mention the number of the quality control people in your operation and the very fact that some stay 24 hours in the factory.

- [ ] Emphasis how profitable will be you counterpart once he decided to perchance your product, you may gain the confidence the counterpart is looking for.

- [ ] Declare your commitment to the products high performance, and above all you should come out with a clear statement per your responsibility for any defect that your counter-part may find in your product once he receives the goods.

- [ ] Do not try to persuade your counterpart for logic approach— rather convince him by showing how your product service meets his needs and desires.

- [ ] Tell your counterpart about your commitment to improve constantly through the education of your quality control people and by investing in new machines to person higher quality of products.

"An avaricious person is like a snake trying to swallow an elephant."

Chinese Proverb (59)

Building Price Structure

Build prices based on these elements:

- ☐ Know the exact price it cost to produce the product. Between the raw material, the production cost, the shipping charges and the overhead.

- ☐ Don't ever over price a quotation, this will fail the prospective buyer and fail you as well. Hence, out yourself victim to the idea of letting your customer get away with at cost price— assuming at the following deals you will compensate yourself. Remember it is hard to increase prices under any objective circumstances.

- ☐ Decide what minimum profit you need to gain from each customer, bug or small.

- ☐ Don't bend to any pressure or promises to get big quantity to sacrifice this price condition. A firm stance behind your price—will reflect your seriousness and intention to provide your counterpart with a quality product.

- ☐ Be acquainted with the market prices in the specific territory you care conducting the negotiation. A competitive price in North Carolina will not sound attractive enough in LA and vice versa.

- ☐ Be familiar with the category in which the customs put your product.

- ☐ Remember time and effort spent during your investigation should influence the direct cost.

"Truth can be outraged by silence, quite as cruelly as by speech."

Amelia Barr

Buyer Response

As you proceed with the product presentation, during those important yet scarce moments—pay attention to the person who is supposed to listen to you.

☐ Pay attention to his gestures and facial expressions. With a basic observation skill you will be able to tell whether your counterpart is sincere. Congruent gestures like touching his face, covering his mouth with his mouth with his fingers, avoiding eye contact, etc—may present a dishonest person. .

☐ Follow his body movement, notice if his eyes are focusing on your face in a way that tells you that he is concentrating on your words. If he is looking at any other direction or staring at the subject in the room—you should know—this person is not interested in you or your product.

☐ Do not hesitate to pack and leave once your counterpart reflects unjustified negative response, remember that you will always fins another opportunity.

☐ Leaving the counterparts office short you are telling him that he has no dignity and you are not wasting time or effort, furthermore, by short cutting the meeting you are giving yourself and extra half-day to check on other prospective partners.

☐ Draw a conclusion you should take one the counter partner inclines to receive phone calls. Hence a sincere partner will instruct his coworker, not to transfer calls till the meeting is over

"The strongest principle of growth lies in human choice."

George Eliot

Market Strategy

At this stage you should express your market distribution and expectation.

- Multi-customer or single customers in a given territory.
- To be a source for existing products as well as developing new ones.

☐ Expect to be asked by a sincere counterpart: "who are you selling to in this town/city?"—a wise and true answer will be "to no one at this stage".

☐ It is preferred to express your willingness to work with one reliable company/customer at a given territory as opposed to few customers.

☐ Avoid selling to any and every customer along a given street—practicing this approach will evoke reluctance and rejection from potential counterparts.

☐ Concentrating—at the early stage—selling to only customers will signal to the counterpart that you have no intention to sell to his direct competitors.

☐ Remember, when you make a concession or offer to the counterpart more than you have planned to do always ask for something in return. If you give a better price structure, ask for a bigger order.

☐ Bear in mind providing he is an honest person, knows quite well he must come with something on his side.

"Success depends in a very large measure upon individuals initiative and exertion, and cannot be achieved except by a dint of hard work."

Anna Pavlova

A Source for Existing Product

To be a source for existing product as well as developing new ones, will draw appreciation and mark an advantage as per the vendors service capability.

- ☐ Offer your counterpart far more than he expected and surprise him by meeting his needs for new products before he ask for it.

- ☐ Be aware that sizable vendors lack the flexibility to come up with new product every so often. On the other hand, vendors with access to new development, styles and innovative designs, new material and applications, will be considered as a great source for any given company.

- ☐ Describe your acquaintances with different Chinese material suppliers. You familiarity with numerous manufactures from which you obtain knowledge about the market trends, new styles and designs.

- ☐ Challenge the counterpart to develop for him any products he needs or sells the most of—in the category of your products to prove your capability.

- ☐ Adopt a strategy to go the extra mile for your counterpart by providing more and better service than he may ask for.

- ☐ Provide answers on solution to new product demands—only if your certain. In case you are not sure, ask to answer your counterpart upon returning back to your office. It will leave a positive impression for quite a long time.

"God sells us all things at the price of labor."

Leonardo D Vinci

The Counterparts Operation

When you are under the impression that the counterpart is satisfied with the most important and relevant answer you have finished him—you may address the counterpart with your set of inquiries.

Purchasing Goods

☐ Ask whether the goods are designated to reach a certain location—that fact will determine the logistics of your shipment method and will have a direct effect on your cost.

☐ Clarify if the goods should be delivered to the warehouse or the nearest port. This applies to the ocean freight expense and the ground transportation expense. Also, it will influence the delivery time.

☐ Prepare to deliver the good only up to the customers port. Being unfamiliar with the process of goods release and brokerage operations and fees it is much better off to leave the counterparts company to take care of releasing the goods from their port.

☐ Avoid by all means the request to ship small quantity of goods by the method of loose cargo. Hence this method invites all kind or irregularity such as involves high fees in comparison to a full container and leave you with a relatively small profit.

☐ Verify the way your counterpart ask for the goods packing and printing. A generic packing and printing of the products has a pre calculated price while a special packing and private label packing involves extra cost.

"Unless you can find some sort of loyalty, you cannot find unity and peace in your active living."

Josaih Royce

Exclusivity

By most part committing to exclusivity for your product/service to one customer is a given territory translate into leaving your freedom of trade and being vulnerable to that customer's mercy. At your early stage of the business in certain territories it is advisable to offer exclusivity on your product to cover 10 to 20 miles radius.

☐ Find out if it is common practice for the buying company to request to be the sole customer in their territory. Some companies will ask it up front—the others will appreciate it if you express your strategy to sell your products to a limited number of customers.

☐ Avoid granting exclusivity if you can get away with it. By the same token do not offer your goods or services to the next customer across the street. Keep a couple of good miles from two prospector companies.

☐ Try to negotiate otherwise. Suggest delaying this commitment to a later stage of your business partnership. It is common to list essential points to the following meeting in anticipation to a better understanding of each side in the near future.

☐ At any given time your commitment to exclusivity should not be one sided reveal your legitimate expectation for serious volume and mutual commitment.

☐ A counterpart with an extended line of products similar to the one you are dealing with should not be offered an exclusivity. The chance for him to purchase from you substantial quantity is rather slim.

"What we see depends mainly on what we look for."

John Lubbock

Placing Orders

You are entitle to ask about the process of purchase orders.
Along processing of issuing the order holds the potential to make
unwanted changes and sometimes even ends up in cancellations of
orders.

☐ Ask to know the entire process of giving the order. Do you
have to fill out endless forma to become a preferred vendor or is
the purchase order issued solely the counterparts responsibility.

☐ Find out the lead time expectation from the moment the
order has been issued until the goods arrive to the port. That
information will prepare and provide you with the accurate
time needs for the first shipment.

☐ It is legitimate and advisable to request estimation per
what realistic volume you can expect to be given at the first
stages and the near future. This information will help you to
prearrange and schedule your factory production line. .

☐ Inquire about any special request per private label since it may
affect the structure of your product and the production time.

☐ Clarify the logistics that are involved in the order. Primarily the
container size, the designated port of arrival, and whether there
is a preferred ocean freight carrier.

"Security depends not so much upon how much you have, as upon how much you can do without."

Joseph Wood Knutch

Terms of Payment

The payment terms issued is a cardinal factor which determines the pace of your company's growth. The cash flow which derives from the smooth payments, control the turnover of your entire operation. In other words, the faster you get aid for the goods you deliver, the more frequent shipments you will be able to maintain.

Letter of Credit

☐ This is the most common mean of payment between import/ export partners. In our case the counterpart is the issuer.

☐ If a letter of credit if offered, one should feel secure. Yet, prepare for substantial amount of paperwork. You might need to be consulted by an office in a commercial bank to take you step by step through the delicate venue so you will be able to read into the terms to make sure to protect your interest.

☐ Reject and request by the counterpart to give him credit line beyond the payment right after the customer receives the goods. You modest cash flow does not leave you with any room to wait for payment ay more than a few days after the goods arrived to the port.

☐ Another method of payment that is practiced if offered to pay in advance—1/3 of the total amount of the value of the goods. Although seldom, it has been granted to new vendors. This suggestion should be blessed since this approach will give you plenty of convince to pay for the production.

"He who cannot endure the bad will not live to see the good."

Jewish Proverb

The Thorny Issue—The Claims

One of the nastiest aspects in the trading is the claim factor. I have mentioned before the tendency among Chinese factory to negligently save on the raw materials. One of the server results occurs out of using inferior material like second grad e glue, used material, fading colors, etc.

☐ Remember—a minor defect in the goods will draw a mild claim of which you as a vendor and the manufacture will be able to handle.

☐ Confronting with defective goods which should be directed to the incinerator and will draw a huge claim that may drag your business for a long time and mark you as an unreliable source/vendor.

☐ Maintain your credibility. Having noticed imperfection quality during the goods production—notify your counterpart immediately. By doing so you reveal integrity and gain the counterparts trust.

☐ Check with the manufacture if he can remake the goods in the quality you wanted in the first place. For it is better to remake the goods (at the manufactures expense) than to compromise on the quality and end up losing your reputation as a reliable source.

☐ In many cases the time factor will not offer you the privilege of remaking the goods, in that case you have to send your counterpart samples for your counterpart to approve the goods before shipment.

"Is is not so much our friends help that helps us, as the confidence of their help."

Epicurus

Asking for a Referral

As you are about to round up the meeting, there is one more thing which is essential to as from your counterpart—a referral. It is used as a legitimate favor to inquire from the counterpart's affiliates or friends who might be a solid candidate for your product.

☐ Ask your counterpart whether he can recommend another prospective buyer from his milieu. A reliable lead as such will shorten a facilitate the road to another trusted counterpart.

☐ In fact—I know from my experience that the very fact when a counterpart is willing to give a referral to introduce you to his colleague who is a decision maker—the chance for you to gain another customer in a short period of time is almost certain.

☐ Granting praise for your personality and your product in front of his colleagues—the counterpart feels obliged to follow suit and execute your business engagement to the better interest of both side.

☐ When you got a referral do not run to cash it before meeting with the new customer. You need to make some study about their geography business environment, since what is good in North Carolina might not be necessarily good in a Florida market.

☐ Keep in mind that your commitment to serve your customer with integrity and professional manner have been extended. Failing to satisfy the referral will affect your business relationship with your counterpart who granted the endorsement.

"We are very near to greatness: one step and we are safe; can we not take the leap?"

Ralph Waldo Emerson

At the Door

Providing you have managed to cover the most essential topics with your counterpart and you fell the foundation of your partnership has been laid down the meeting is concluded. It is time to hit the road.

☐ The samples you have bought with you should be offered to your counterpart for evaluation and reference. The counterpart may need to bring them to his colleagues for a team consultation. .

☐ Make sure you keep a duplicate set of your samples to follow future inquires. Loosing track per what style, color, price, etc.—will bring the entire contract to square 1.

☐ You have to thank the counterpart for the opportunity to present your merchandise, promise to follow up regarding the issues that were discussed. Remember a meeting without follow up will signal to the counterpart your unprofessional attitude or let him think you ended up conducting business with his competitor.

☐ Shake hands firmly and express your impression that this meeting makes a beginning of a long business relationship. A sincere positive attitude tends to inspire the counterpart.

☐ On your way out it is strongly suggested to ask the person at the reception area their name and express your gratitude. You definitely need this front line assistance once you resume the contact.

"Even if you are on the right track, you'll get run over if you just sit there."

Will Rogers

Back To The Hotel

Reaching back to your hotel room spend some time documenting the important topics discussed during the meeting. Open your notebook and start filling up all those notes you could not write at the counterpart's presence.

☐ Write down all relevant questions/answers that have been exchanged, the counterparts comments, excitements, etc. Back at home these notes will serve you beautifully to diagnose the texture of your meeting.

☐ Providing you have set a second appointment, it is advisably to be tens of miles away from another. You should conduct that meeting in the same manner as the first one.

☐ It will be to your benefit to reveal the name of the company you have just visited, furthermore, assuming you have met with a respectable company, your second counterpart will greet you with respect for the prospective customer you are dealing with and more so for your sincere approach.

☐ Do not hide a previous meeting, it will be revealed by the counterpart sometime down the line. This will draw a suspicious attitude. Although the United States is a huge country, the industry is very well communicated and informed.

☐ Three to five meetings should be the desirable number of encounters during your first trip. The follow up on those meetings should be treated with devotion.

"If I had six hours to chop down a tree, I'd spend the first hour sharpening the ax."

Abraham Lincoln

Chapter 6

Follow Up

Back To Your Office

Though assuming you have met with 3 sizable wholesalers, a thorough attitude will be needed to cover the specific request from each of the prospective counterparts. Details like specs relating the product you have offered; colors, shipping information, product lead time, and samples consumed or requested, concentration, and time.

☐ Samples you have promised to the counterpart should be executed in no time. A courier method of shipping should be adopted, since most counterparts expect a prompt response from you and it reflects your seriousness.

☐ Send a thank you letter to the counterpart a few days after your meeting to thank them for spending time with you. It is essential to keep in touch with the counterpart within 2 weeks from the time of your initial meeting.

☐ Try to supply all samples your counterpart asked for, however, only perfect samples that can be produced and manufacture maintaining the same quality. Only those samples should be sent.

☐ All the information and details you promise to give him should be elaborate and sent to him promptly. Be accurate on the information and check thoroughly with the factory before you commit to an answer.

☐ It is far better to send a moderate quality samples and to surprise the counterpart with high quality during mass production.

"People are lucky and unlucky—according to the ratio between what they get and what they have been led to expect."

Samuel Butler

The Nature of Responses

There are a couple of typical responses you may encounter from which you will draw your next move.

- Ignoring.
- Time request for reevaluation.
- Positive response.

☐ **Ignoring**: The highest probability and the most disappointing encounter is no response at all. A disturbing silence.

☐ Check your shipping/sailing record to verify whether the material has been sent to the counterpart has been received by his office.

☐ Providing the material/samples have reached its destination at least 2 weeks ago, there is room to call on the counterpart and to inquire—firmly yet politely—for their response. Failing to reach him, leave a phone message and keep trying.

☐ Give a grace of one week if there is still no reaction from the counterpart. Send him an email in which you express desire to hear from them.

☐ A complete silence is unacceptable. Call their office operation/reception's extension and enquire about their absence sue to short leave, trip, vacation, etc.

☐ Experiencing shortcoming answers from the counterpart should tell you that the prospective buyer needs to be left alone—at least for the time being.

"When written in Chinese, the word "Crisis" is composed of two characters. One represents danger and the other represents opportunity."

John F Kennedy

Request for Reevaluation

Sometime you will find that your counterpart is objectively in need of X amount of time to finalize a response. The objectively comprises of a couple of factors:

☐ Company policy.

☐ A counterparts response in this nature should be accepted with respect and patience. However, it is highly recommended to contact that counterpart every 3-3 weeks to keep the line secure and alive.

☐ Reveal to them about your current business activity and expose your new product (send emails with picture and specs of preferably actual samples).

☐ IN case you have not heard back from your buyer for 2-3 months there is room to call on the gatekeeper to find out if he is still with the company. Changing position or company all together is common practice in the U.S market.

☐ You can wait up to 2-3 month to have the counterpart on board and actually detailing the first purchase order. If at that period nothing has materialized, that should translate as "not interested and you should give up" on the prospective buyer.

☐ Remember—time material, and energy should be diverted to other potential counterparts but do not burn that bridge—you might meet up again someday.

"I studied the lives of great men and famous woman; and I found that the men and woman who got to the top were those who did the jobs they had in hand, with everything they had of energy and enthusiasm and hard work."

Harry S. Truman

A Positive Response

This is the avenue you put you out most. Here is the beginning of your real business, you are giving and opportunity, and you should put your best efforts forward and not blow it. The American counterpart is giving you business "go ahead" after subduing a mouth of hesitance, fear of the unknown, and a lot of objective obstacle. Treat this opportunity as your first and last one.

- ☐ Do not come short to your commitment on material, quality, lead time, and delivery will result in losing the counterpart as a customer. You can only dream about the second chance.

- ☐ Pay attention and it is necessary to be on top of each step of the order execution choosing the right factory, selecting the proper material, supervising the production steps, and go thoroughly thru the inspection and deliver goods on time.

- ☐ In order to gain respect of the counterpart go the extra mil e and address you product in the American fashion. Use the best material to emphasize quality in every way, even though it means less profit.

- ☐ Remember—low grade material will invite claims and sever the relationship. While good quality material brings more orders.

- ☐ Providing your goods shipments reach the counterparts warehouse in fine condition. Here is the proper time to inquire payment, Make sure you follow the agreed terms of payment in a very strict manner,.

"Then give the world the best you have and the rest will come back to you."

Madeline Bridges

Acknowledgements

Thanks to:

My wife Aviva Eyal who contributed wise advice from her personal business encounters with the oriental markets.

Mr. Johnny Chen my Chinese business partner who went along with me through a period of ten years to understand his experience in dealing with western traders.

Mr. C.C. Wang the professor in Sho-Schow University in Taipe for teaching me the fundamental aspects of the Chinese business approach.

Mr. Ezra Anzaruth, a dear family friend and partner for contributing from his east west trading experience.